OUTDOOR SPACES

OUTDOOR SPACES

Ana G. Cañizares

COLLINS | DESIGN

An Imprint of HarperCollins*Publishers*

HarperCollins books may be purchased for educational, business, or sales promotional use.
For information, please write: Special Markets Department, HarperCollins Publishers Inc.,
10 East 53rd Street, New York, NY 10022.

English language edition first published in 2006 by:
Collins Design
An Imprint of HarperCollins*Publishers*
10 East 53rd Street
New York, NY 10022
Tel.: (212) 207-7000
Fax: (212) 207-7654
collinsdesign@harpercollins.com
www.harpercollins.com

Distributed throughout the world by:
HarperCollins*Publishers*
10 East 53rd Street
New York, NY 10022
Fax: (212) 207-7654

Packaged by:
Loft Publications
Via Laietana, 32 4°, of. 92
08003 Barcelona, Spain
Tel.: +34 932 688 088
Fax: +34 932 687 073
www.loftpublications.com

Editor: Ana G. Cañizares
Art Director: Mireia Casanovas Soley
Layout: Nacho Gracia Blanco

Library of Congress Control Number: 2006922656

Printed in by: Anman Gràfiques de Vallès
DL: B-10866-06
First Printing, 2006

CONTENTS

Introduction

Humans have always had a unique bond with nature, one that has been unfortunately weakened by the growth of densely populated urban centers. The earliest examples of dwellings incorporated exterior spaces into the home, designed for cooking, cleaning, and resting. Today, the integration of outdoor spaces is an attempt to re-establish this connection with the outdoors. Considered a privilege, especially in large cities, the access to an outdoor space within the privacy of a residence can be taken advantage of in many ways. Terraces, balconies, gardens, and courtyards can be transformed, no matter what their size, into relaxing spaces in which to unwind or as sources of light that can filter in to the interior spaces of the residence. Through the use of the appropriate materials, furnishings, plants, colors, textures, and other accessories, an outdoor space can become a genuine oasis in any private home. *Outdoor Spaces* gathers an extensive selection of innovative projects by contemporary architects and landscape designers. They shed light on ways to make the most of an outdoor space, to strengthen the relationship between the interior and exterior and to improve the quality of our lives.

Architect: **Unknown**
Photography: © **Montse Garriga**
Location: **Spain**

TERRACES & BALCONIES

Their ability to adapt to any type of residence and their relatively low maintenance make terraces the most versatile type of exterior space. They can take the form of balconies, verandas, porches, decks, or patios, and can be situated on the ground, on the roof, or cantilevered over another level. The character of a terrace is generally determined by the location in which it is set. City terraces, for example, are often more introverted due to the density of the urban fabric, the proximity of neighboring terraces, and occasionally, unpleasant views. For this reason, urban terraces tend to provide a framework that captures the most interesting available views. They also seek privacy through the use of natural elements such as hedges, thick shrubs, and tall trees, which also serve as a protective visual and acoustic barrier. Rural terraces, on the other hand, typically enjoy a far more direct relationship with the landscape, integrating lounges, play areas, dining rooms, and even cooking areas that merge with the surrounding vegetation and embrace scenic views. Large or small, covered or open, these spaces can be converted from dull, useless areas to practical and comfortable spaces in which to relax and enjoy the climate.

Architect: **Gaterman & Schossig**
Photography: © **Robertino Nikolic**
Location: **Cologne, Germany**

Architect: **Josep Juvé**
Photography: © **Eugeni Pons**
Location: **Sant Sadurní d'Anoia, Spain**

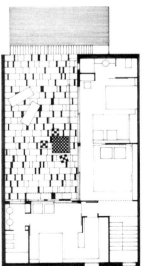

First floor

Architect: **Dangar Group**
Photography: © **Murray Fredericks**
Location: **St. Ives, Australia**

Architect: **Ian Chee & Voon Wong**
Photography: © **Henry Wilson/Redcover.com**
Location: **London, UK**

Architect: **R. Thomson**
Photography: © **Andrew Twort/Redcover.com**
Location: **Oxford, UK**

Architect: **Unknown**
Photography: © **Ricardo Labougle**
Location: **Punta del Este, Uruguay**

Architect: **Unknown**
Photography: © **Montse Garriga**
Location: **Spain**

Architect: **dosAdos Arquitectura del Paisatge**
Photography: © **Gogortza/Llorella**
Location: **Barcelona, Spain**

Architect: **Marcio Kogan**
Photography: © **Arnaldo Pappalardo**
Location: **Sao Paulo, Brazil**

Architect: **Susan Petch**
Photography: © **Dan Magree**
Location: **Victoria, Australia**

Architect: **Habitus Architects**
Photography: © **Dan Magree**
Location: **Victoria, Australia**

Architect: **SORG Architects**
Photography: © **Robert Lautman & Steven Ahlgren**
Location: **Sherwood, MD, USA**

Architect: **Unknown**
Photography: © **Jordi Miralles**
Location: **Spain**

■ Architect: **Unknown**
Photography: © **Montse Garriga**
Location: **Spain**

Architect: **Unknown**
Photography: © **Montse Garriga**
Location: **Spain**

Architect: **Unknown**
Photography: © Montse Garriga
Location: **Spain**

Architect: **Samuel Lerch**
Photography: © **Bruno Helbling/Zapaimages**
Location: **Kuessnacht, Switzerland**

Architect: **Björn Conerdings**
Photography: **Reto Guntli/Zapaimages**
Location: **Marrakesh, Morocco**

Architect: **Studio Bau:ton**
Photography: © **John Ellis**
Location: **Pacific Palisades, CA, USA**

Architect: **Ettorre Sottsass**
Photography: **© Undine Pröhl**
Location: **California, USA**

■ Architect: **Patrick Clifford, Bowes Clifford Thomson**
Photography: © **Patrick Reynolds**
Location: **Medlands Beach, Gran Barrier Island, New Zealand**

■ Architect: **LMS Architects**
Photography: © **Undine Pröhl**
Location: **San Francisco, CA, USA**

Architect: **Unknown**
Photography: © **Montse Garriga**
Location: **Spain**

Architect: **Prima Design**
Photography: © **Giorgio Baroni**
Location: **New York, NY, USA**

Architect: **Unknown**
Photography: © **Jordi Miralles**
Location: **Barcelona, Spain**

Architect: **Barclay & Carousse**
Photography: © **Barclay & Carousse**
Location: **Cañete, Peru**

Architect: **dosAdos Arquitectura del Paisatge**
Photography: **© Gogortza/Llorella**
Location: **Sitges, Spain**

■ Architect: **Cha & Innerhofer**
Photography: **© Dao Lou Zha**
Location: **New York, NY, USA**

Top floor

Architect: **Miller Hull Partnership**
Photography: © **James Housel**
Location: **Seattle, WA, USA**

Architect: **Álvaro Siza**
Photography: © **Duccio Malagamba**
Location: **Porto, Portugal**

Top floor

■ Architect: **Anne Marie Sumner**
Photography: © **Nelson Kon**
Location: **Ubatuba, Brazil**

Architect: **Graftworks Architecture & Design**
Photography: © **David Joseph**
Location: **New York, NY, USA**

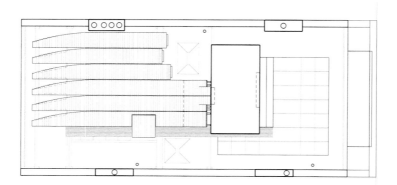

Roof plan

Architect: **Magín Ruiz de Albornoz**
Photography: © **Joan Roig**
Location: **Valencia, Spain**

■ Architect: **Rios Clementi Hale Studios**
Photography: © **John Ellis**
Location: **Brentwood, CA, USA**

■ Architect: **Miro Rovira Architects**
Photography: © **Patrick Wong**
Location: **Austin, TX, USA**

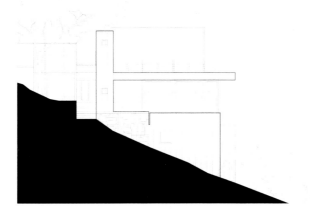

Elevation

Architect: **Jyrki Tasa**
Photography: © **Jyrki Tasa**
Location: **Espoo, Finland**

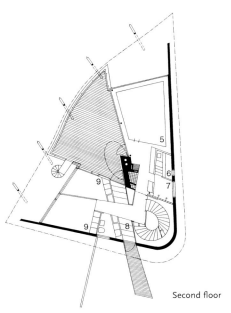

Second floor

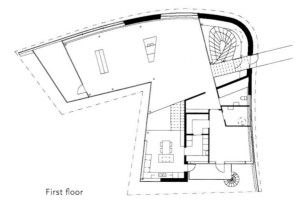

First floor

Architect: **Nurmela-Raimoranta-Tasa Architects**
Photography: © Jyrki Tasa, Jussi Tianen
Location: **Espoo, Finland**

Architect: **Hans Peter Wörndl**
Photography: © **Paul Ott**
Location: **Vienna, Austria**

Architect: **Jamie Loft**
Photography: © **Shania Shegedyn**
Location: **Sydney, Australia**

Architect: **Jamie Loft**
Photography: © **Shania Shegedyn**
Location: **Sydney, Australia**

■ Architect: **Harry Seidler & Associates**
Photography: © **Eric Sierins**
Location: **Joadja, Australia**

■ Architect: **Enea Garden Design**
Photography: © **Sabrina Rothe/Artur**
Location: **Zurich, Switzerland**

Architect: **Frederick Fisher**
Photography: © **Undine Pröhl**
Location: **Venice, CA, USA**

Architect: **Safdie Rabines Architects**
Photography: © **Undine Pröhl**
Location: **Mission Hills, CA, USA**

■ Architect: **Charles Deaton/Praxis Design**
Photography: © **Undine Pröhl**
Location: **California, USA**

Architect: **Emili Fox**
Photography: © **Eric Sierens**
Location: **Sydney, Australia**

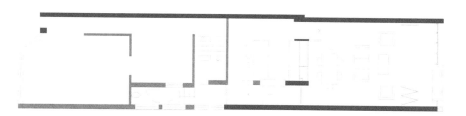

Floor plan

■ Architect: **Callas Shortridge Architects**
Photography: **© Undine Pröhl**
Location: **Pacific Palisades, CA, USA**

Architect: **Shubin & Donaldson Architects**
Photography: **© Tom Bonner**
Location: **Malibu, CA, USA**

Architect: **Innocad**
Photography: © **Paul Ott, Graz**
Location: **Graz, Austria**

Second floor

■ Architect: **Grady Cooley**
Photography: **© Andreas von Einsiedel**
Location: **London, UK**

Architect: **BBP Architects**
Photography: **© Chris Ott**
Location: **Melbourne, Australia**

Third floor

Fourth floor

Architect: **Derek Dellekamp/Dellekamp Arquitectos**
Photography: © **Oscar Necoechea, Lara Becerra**
Location: **Mexico DF, Mexico**

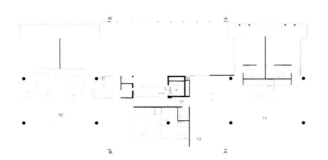

Fourth floor

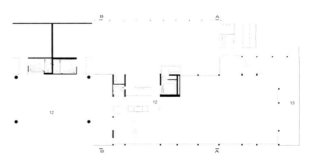

Fifth floor

Elevation

■ Architect: **Ramón Fernández-Alonso Borrajo**
Photography: **© Fernando Alda**
Location: **Granada, Spain**

Third floor

Architect: **Despacho Boncompte-Font, Diego Scaglia**
Photography: **© Eugeni Pons**
Location: **Lloret de Mar, Spain**

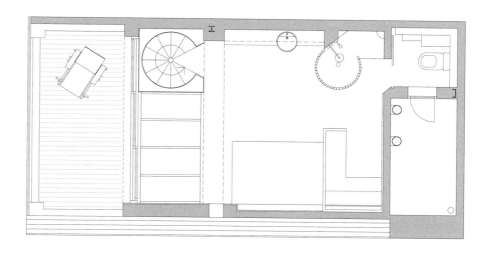

Second floor

First floor

■ Architect: **Alberto Martínez Carbajal**
Photography: **© Jordi Miralles**
Location: **Barcelona, Spain**

Architect: **Marc Egerton**
Photography: © **Miquel Tres**
Location: **Sitges, Spain**

■ Architect: **Jean Bocabeille & Ignacio Prego**
Photography: © **Ken Hayden/Redcover.com**
Location: **Milos, Greece**

COURTYARDS

Located in the center of a residential plan, a courtyard is open to the outdoors. At the same time, it is enclosed, granting privacy and silence and providing daylight to a home's interior spaces. Its close relationship to the interior makes a courtyard a versatile space that can be used to define the passage from private to public zones or to carry out a wide range of functions given the intimacy that it affords. In addition, courtyards, unlike open terraces or gardens, can offer protection from the wind while maintaining an optimum level of ventilation. These innate characteristics, together with an imaginative use of space and materials, can transform courtyards into singular environments that combine the benefits of the outdoors as well as the advantages of an interior space.

Architect: **Akira Sakamoto**
Photography: © **Yoshiharu Matsumura**
Location: **Kashiba, Japan**

■ Architect: **Faulkner & Chapman Landscape Design**
Photography: **© Shania Shegedyn**
Location: **Brighton, Australia**

Architect: **Terence Conran**
Photography: © **Ken Hayden/Redcover.com**
Location: **London, UK**

Architect: **Landau & Kindelbacher**
Photography: © **Michael Heinrich**
Location: **Munich, Germany**

■ Architect: **Guillermo Arias & Luis Cuartas**
Photography: © **Eduardo Consuegra**
Location: **Honda, Colombia**

156

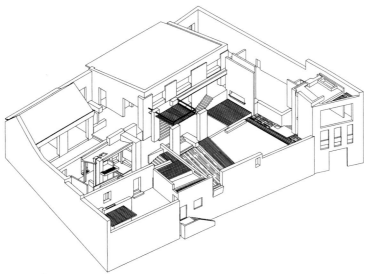

Architect: **Unknown**
Photography: © **Montse Garriga**
Location: **Tarragona, Spain**

Architect: **Unknown**
Photography: **©** **Ricardo Labougle**
Location: **Buenos Aires, Argentina**

Architect: **Candy & Candy**
Photography: **© Andreas von Einsiedel**
Location: **London, UK**

Architect: **Niels Hansen**
Photography: © **Andreas von Einsiedel**
Location: **Majorca, Spain**

■ Architect: **Alberto Burckhardt**
Photography: © **Alberto Burckhardt, Beatriz Santo Domingo**
Location: **Bogotá, Colombia**

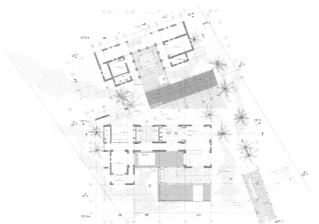

Ground floor

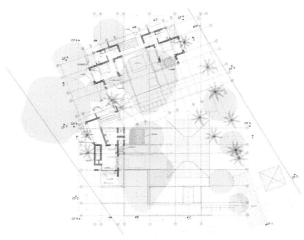

First floor

■ Architect: **Culti**
Photography: **© Giulio Oriani/Vega MG**
Location: **Ostuni, Italy**

Architect: **Carles Gelpí i Arroyo**
Photography: **© Eugeni Pons**
Location: **Barcelona, Spain**

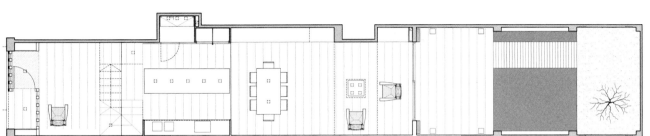

Ground floor

Architect: **Mamen Domingo & Ernest Ferré Arquitectes**
Photography: © **Jovan Horvath**
Location: **Reus, Spain**

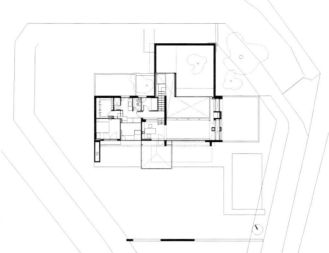

Floor plan

■ Architect: **Eduardo Souto de Moura**
Photography: © **Duccio Malagamba**
Location: **Porto, Portugal**

Architect: **Jaime Sanahuja**
Photography: © **Joan Roig**
Location: **Oropesa del Mar, Spain**

Ground floor

Architect: **Josep Lluís Mateo/Map Architect**
Photography: **© Duccio Malagamba**
Location: **Barcelona, Spain**

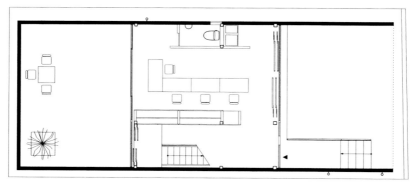

Ground floor

Architect: **Junya Toda Architects & Associates**
Photography: © **Miyogi Uedga**
Location: **Osaka, Japan**

■ Architect: **David Giovannitti**
Photography: © **Michael Moran**
Location: **New York, NY, USA**

Architect: **GCA Arquitectes Associats**
Photography: © **Jordi Miralles**
Location: **Barcelona, Spain**

Floor plan

Architect: **Zack de Vito Architecture**
Photography: © **Massimiliano Bozonella**
Location: **San Francisco, CA, USA**

Floor plan

Architect: **Stefania Rinaldi/Studio Rinaldi**
Photography: **© Wade Zimmerman**
Location: **New York, NY, USA**

Architect: **Jaume Prior**
Photography: © **Joan Roig**
Location: **Nules, Spain**

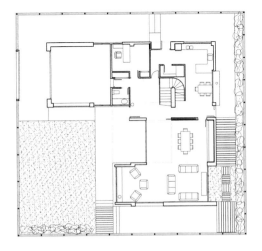

Floor plan

■ Architect: **Richard Kerr Architecture**
Photography: © **Derek Swalwell**
Location: **Melbourne, Australia**

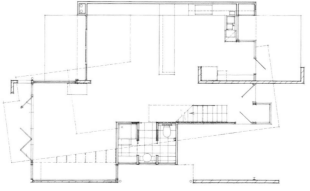

Ground floor

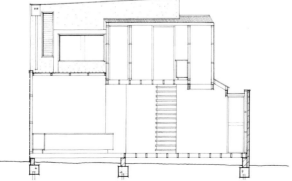

Section

Architect: **Massimo Sottili**
Photography: © **Gianni Basso/Vega MG**
Location: **Milan, Italy**

Floor plan

Architect: **MCP Arquitectura**
Photography: © **Joan Roig**
Location: **Massalfassar, Spain**

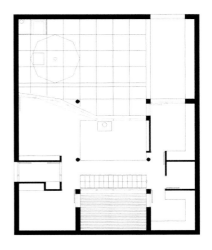

Floor plan

■ Architect: **Pedro López García**
Photography: © **David Frutos**
Location: **Espinardo, Spain**

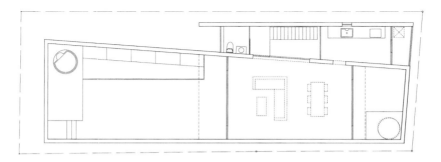

Floor plan

Architect: **Satoshi Okada Architects**
Photography: © **Satoshi Okada Architects**
Location: **Sakakida, Japan**

Architect: **Studio Associato Falconi**
Photography: © **Gianni Basso/Vega MG**
Location: **Brescia, Italy**

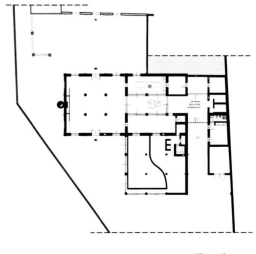

Floor plan

Architect: **Verdickt & Verdickt Architecten**
Photography: © **Giorgio Possenti/Vega MG**
Location: **Antwerp, Belgium**

Architect: **Ibarra Rosano Design Architects**
Photography: © **Bill Timmerman**
Location: **Tucson, AZ, USA**

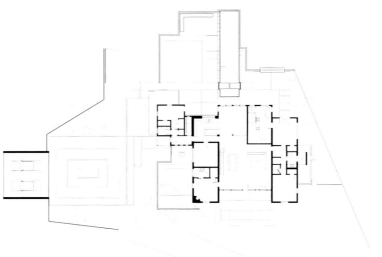

Floor plan

Architect: **Taylor Cullity Lethlean**
Photography: © **Ben Wrigley**
Location: **Melbourne, Australia**

Architect: **Matt Gibson A + D**
Photography: **© John Wheatley**
Location: **Victoria, Australia**

Architect: **David Hertz Architects**
Photography: © **David Hertz**
Location: **Venice, CA, USA**

Architect: **Tezuka Architects, Masahiro Ikeda**
Photography: © **Katsuhisa Kida**
Location: **Tokyo, Japan**

Architect: **Michelle Kauffman**
Photography: **© Sunset Magazine**
Location: **Prefab**

Floor plan

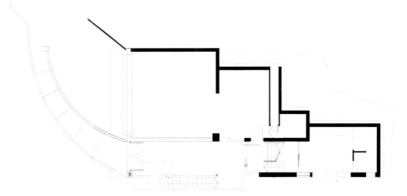

Ground floor

▪ Architect: **Molnar Freeman Architects**
Photography: © **Murray Fredericks**
Location: **Sydney, Australia**

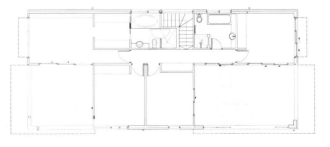

Third floor

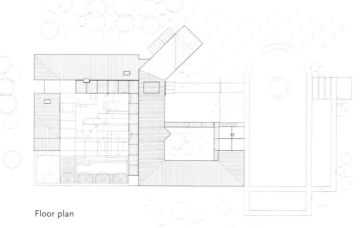

Floor plan

Architect: **Carlos Jiménez Studio**
Photography: © **Paul Hester, Hester & Hardaway Photography**
Location: **Marfa, TX, USA**

Architect: **Fabricio Leoni Architettura**
Photography: © **Dessi Monari**
Location: **Sardinia, Italy**

Interior Designer: **Fàtima Vilaseca**
Photography: © **Jordi Miralles**
Location: **Cerdanya, Spain**

Landscape Architect: **Maria Ros, Ignacio Poch**
Photography: © **Montse Garriga**
Location: **Girona, Spain**

GARDENS

The private garden has existed as long as architecture has, and has always been perceived as a space that provides the thrill of exerting control over nature while recreating natural processes within the home. Today gardens can exist in very small spaces as long as the conditions allow and the appropriate elements are chosen. With the proper care and attention, an adequate selection of plants in relation to the temperature, the amount of light, and the type of soil can result in a flourishing garden. In addition, new interpretations of the traditional garden provide greater freedom in terms of materials and room for experimentation. This evolving trend has given way to original designs that integrate plants, water, furniture, and architectural elements such as concrete planters or paved walkways, generating gardens that are increasingly interesting and varied.

Architect: **AV62 Arquitectos**
Photography: © **Eugeni Pons**
Location: **Plentzia, Spain**

Architect: **Lluís Auqué**
Photography: **© Montse Garriga**
Location: **Girona, Spain**

Architect: **Pilar Libano**
Photography: © **Montse Garriga**
Location: **Girona, Spain**

Architect: **Kate Pols**
Photography: **© Andreas von Einsiedel**
Location: **Hampshire, UK**

Architect: **Dry Design**
Photography: **© Undine Pröhl**
Location: **Santa Monica, CA, USA**

Architect: **Unknown**
Photography: **© Jon Bouchier/Redcover.com**
Location: **London, UK**

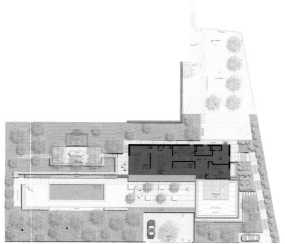

Floor plan

Architect: **Raderschall**
Photography: © **Raderschall**
Location: **Zurich, Switzerland**

Architect: **Andrea Cochran**
Photography: © **Andrea Cochran**
Location: **Palo Alto, CA, USA**

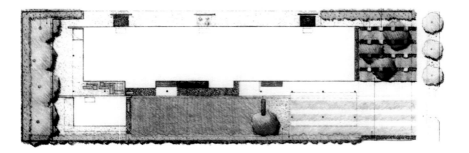

Floor plan

Architect: **Out From The Blue, Mira Marinazzo**
Photography: © **Shania Shegedyn**
Location: **Melbourne, Australia**

Architect: **Out From The Blue, Loredana Ducco**
Photography: **©** **Shania Shegedyn**
Location: **Melbourne, Australia**

Architect: **Unknown**
Photography: © **Montse Garriga**
Location: **Spain**

Architect: **Felipe Assadi Figueroa**
Photography: © **Juan Purcell**
Location: **Calera de Tango, Chile**

Architect: **Alfons Argila**
Photography: © **Miquel Tres**
Location: **Sitges, Spain**

Architect: **Ricard Farrés**
Photography: © **Miquel Tres**
Location: **Sabadell, Spain**

Architect: **CCS Architecture**
Photography: © **CCS Architecture, JD Peterson**
Location: **Sonoma, CA, USA**

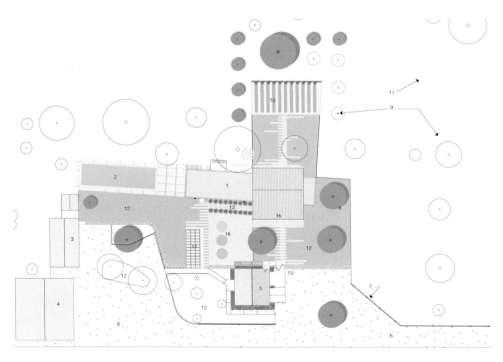

Floor plan

Architect: **Marmol Radziner & Associates**
Photography: © **Tim Street-Porter**
Location: **Palm Springs, CA, USA**

Architect: **Groep Delta Architectur**
Photography: © **Groep Delta Architectuur**
Location: **Hasselt, Belgium**

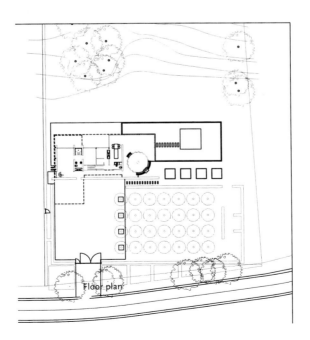

Floor plan

Architect: **Emulsion Architecture**
Photography: **© Leon Chew**
Location: **London, UK**

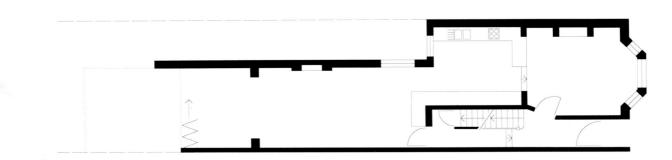

Floor plan

Floor plan

Architect: **Rotzler Krebs Partner**
Photography: © **Rotzler Krebs Partner**
Location: **Wollerau, Switzerland**

Architect: **dosAdos Arquitectura del Paisatge**
Photography: © **Gogortza/Llorella**
Location: **Tiana, Spain**

Architect: **Landau & Kindelbacher**
Photography: © **R & R Hackl, Landshut**
Location: **Munich, Germany**

Architect: **Bernhard Korte**
Photography: © **Sabrina Rothe/Artur**
Location: **Cologne, Germany**

Architect: **Dardelet**
Photography: © **Dardelet**
Location: **Winkel, Switzerland**

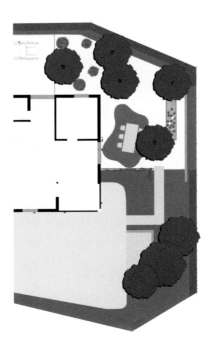

Floor plan

Architect: **RCR Arquitectes, Francisco Asensio Cerver**
Photography: **© Roger Casas**
Location: **Barcelona, Spain**